Amos R Wells

Nutshell Musings

Quiet Moments With the Word of God

Amos R Wells

Nutshell Musings
Quiet Moments With the Word of God

ISBN/EAN: 9783337088279

Printed in Europe, USA, Canada, Australia, Japan

Cover: Foto ©Lupo / pixelio.de

More available books at **www.hansebooks.com**

Nutshell Musings

Quiet Moments with
the Word of God . .

BY

AMOS R. WELLS

Author of " When Thou Hast Shut Thy Door,"
" Sunday-School Success," etc.

NEW YORK   CHICAGO   TORONTO
Fleming H. Revell Company
Publishers of Evangelical Literature

Preface

THE Bible is verily a tree of life. Upon its gracious boughs hangs fruit of all kinds, suited to all needs. Moreover, it is fruitful at all times, in sad hours and happy hours alike, at seasons of failure or doubt or prosperity. No one ever came to it hungry and went empty away.

The following pages present a handful of its fruit, gathered with delight, and offered with confidence, for the fruit is none of mine. Mary "thought He was the gardener." He *is* the Gardener.

This is the *Quiet Hour Series* of books. Doubtless nothing is more needed by our nervous age than quiet hours with the Great Teacher. We are in danger of losing the strong art of meditation. It is not the half-hour of eating that counts, but the hours of digestion; not the bit of

Preface

Bible food hastily snatched, but the musing upon it. May this book of meditations upon Bible texts, most of them passages not commonly thought upon, aid to some degree the growth of this fruitful practice.

Amos R. Wells.

Boston, August, 1899.

Contents

Contents

" While I was musing the fire burned."—*Psa.* xxxix. 3.

For the Shut-Ins

"And the Lord shut him in."—*Gen.* vii. 16.

TO be shut in by God is better than to be given by men the freedom of all cities and the range of all lands. God never shuts in except as He shut Noah in. The prison is always an ark, and God's prisoners are always prisoners of hope. Their prison is lifted on high by the floods of woe, and left on a mountain-top. God's shut-ins always come out on a higher level than they went in.

And whenever God shuts a man in, just as when He shut Noah in, He sends to the prison all the kinds of life that could be met in the widest possible journeyings. Two by two, male and female, for mating and increase, beast and bird filed into the ark. All creation flows toward God's shut-ins. The chamber may be narrow,

For the Shut-Ins

but it has room for the widest experiences. Heroisms find ample scope there. On a field no larger than a counterpane all the virtues and powers can perform their evolutions. Within close confining walls discoveries may be made that dwarf the researches of a Stanley. Types of all happenings, all conquests and achievements, find entrance to God's arks.

Happy is the soul that remains obedient and contented in His prison till it has found its Ararat, till the blessed Dove gives the token, and God opens the door of release !

The Test of Memory

" Can a maid forget her ornaments, or a bride her attire ? yet My people have forgotten Me days without number."—*Jer.* ii. 32.

YOU are known to God not by what you remember, but by what you cannot forget. You are able to remember your Bible-reading, but you are also able to forget it. God will know you as a Bible-reader when you *cannot help* remembering it, because you love it. You can remember to say your prayers, but prayer has not become the inevitable, the longed for, the delight. While it is possible for you to forget to pray, God knows that you are not a prayer-lover.

Do not allow yourself to be misled by your duty-doing. Estimate yourself by your instincts. Not that duty is not to be done, if not by instinct, then by self-compulsion ; but the end is not that the duty may get done, but that it may get instinctive.

Religion must become your ornament, the diamond that glitters on your finger, so that you like to look at your hand ; the rose in your hair, held by a jewelled clasp ; the shining charm of everything you do. "No learning goes where there's no pleasure ta'en," says the greatest of secular writers. There is little use in reading a book that is not pleasing to you. And thus, also, must religion be attractive to you before it can hold you, before you can be religious.

Whenever the church is feeble, whenever Christians are flaccid, it is because men have been content with remembering God, instead of going on to the impossibility of forgetting Him.

Empty Houses

" Ye have built houses of hewn stone, but ye shall not dwell in them."—*Amos* **v. 11.**

OH, the waste of carpenter work and mason work in this world ! Not half the houses that are built are ever lived in.

There's Tryphena Trifler's education— a costly mansion, that made her father's pocketbook sweat, I assure you. But she never moved in. Her talk since commencement day has been all of beaux and bonnets, and her thoughts of ribbons and lace and her own pretty face.

Then, there's Sam Selfish's marriage. A pearl of a home it should have made him, with his Susan, as lovely of soul as of features. Alas, it is an empty house, as poor Susan's pale cheeks show; for there's only one drayman that can move a man into his marriage—Mr. Love. And Sam Selfish has no use for *him*.

Worst of all, there's Will Worldly's church-membership. Why, it is a regular palace, with large promise windows, and service doors that are heavy but lordly, and all the furniture of happiness. But Will has never moved in. The house stands to his name on the books, and that is all the good it does him.

There's nothing more sad than an empty house. Have you any on your life estate?

Stocks and Trees

"Shall I fall down to the stock of a tree?"—
Isa. xliv. 19.

THE essence of idolatry is its stock-iness, its deadness. It takes green trees and cuts them up into wooden posts that rot away. For our idols are made from great fundamental desires and pleasures, which, so long as they are rooted and grounded in Christ, are good trees, bringing forth good fruit. It is the axe of selfishness that cuts them down, and makes from them idols, dead and deadening.

Wealth is a great palm, while it is used for Christ; but as soon as it is used for self, its beautiful branches fall away, it becomes a stock. Beauty is a graceful elm, while it is held as a gift from Christ; but as soon as it is prostituted to self, its leaves wither and decay sets in. Power is a magnificent oak, while its roots go down deep in Christ ; but as soon as it ceases to be at Christ's command, its strength is level with the dust. Knowledge is a richly laden apple-tree, while the harvest is Christ's ; but when it is dedicated to any other service than His, it bears only apples of Sodom. So with talents, so with fame, so with good fortune, so with influence among men, so with everything good the world ever possessed,—it may be a green tree, or it may be a stock.

And shall I fall down to the stock of a tree ?

Would You Be Satisfied?

" But unto the tribe of Levi, Moses gave not any inheritance: the Lord God of Israel was their inheritance, as He said unto them."—*Josh.* xiii. 33.

WHAT a daring thing for Moses to do,—to divide the land among the other tribes, but to give the Levites no inheritance save "the Lord God of Israel"!

I wonder if all the Levites were pleased. I wonder if any of them thought that Reuben and Gad or Manasseh, receiving their shares of the Promised Land, had the best of the bargain. If so, that disappointed Levite got no inheritance at all, neither that of the Levites, nor that of the other eleven tribes; neither land, nor God.

And if you had been in the place of the Levites, would *you* have been satisfied?

You *are* in their place. You have the opportunity of their inheritance. The

Would You Be Satisfied?

Lord God of Israel will be your inheritance, if you choose.

You do not object, but you want *also* a piece of the land flowing with milk and honey? No; you cannot serve God and mammon. It is one or the other.

But might not God have been the inheritance of the Benjamite or the Reubenite as well as of the Levite? Certainly, if he really counted God better than all other possessions and was ready to prove it by giving up all other possessions, if need be.

But would not the Levites have fared a little better if, in addition to having God, they had been assigned to a share of the land? No; for they *had* all the land and all lands, having the God of all lands. Which would you choose from a king, a county, or to be adopted as the king's son?

Now God will give the supreme Gift, "the unspeakable Gift," to no man who will not, to obtain it, "sell all that he hath." Will you? Nay, in your eager readiness *have* you already?

Your Kingdom

"And the kingdom and dominion, and the greatness of the kingdom under the whole heaven, shall be given to the people of the saints of the Most High."—*Dan.* vii. 27.

THIS is true; and whoever believes it is thereby emancipated from half the worries of life—those that spring from the desire to "get on in the world." All our "getting on," in this world or in any other, depends upon this one thing, upon our being saints of the Most High.

You with your furrowed brow and your restless, anxious heart,—you are digging for potatoes close beside a field rich in gold nuggets; you are leaping for a fool's cap while a crown is within your grasp; you are madly pursuing Sorrow although Joy is stretching after you an appealing hand; you are seeking the paltry, time-dwarfed, and body-bound kingdoms of this world, while there is waiting for you to claim it the kingdom and the dominion, and the greatness of the kingdom, under the whole heaven. You have only to be one of God's saints.

But that is not easy. Of course it is not easy, or with such a prize in so clear view who of us would fail to seek it? Given equal powers of mind, and a man might become twenty emperors rather than one saint. Good is not given away. Sainthood needs more toil than kinghood.

But it is toil in which God helps. His is the kingdom and the power and the glory forever, and they are His with the one eager purpose that He may share them with as many as will take them on His terms. If we can bear what He bears, we may sit with Him on His throne.

Gadders

"Why gaddest thou about so much?"—*Jer.* ii. 36.

HE dictionary derives the word *gad* from an Irish word meaning to steal, to pilfer. A suitable ancestry. The man that gads about does nothing but pilfer,—from other folks, but chiefly from himself.

I was thinking about church-gadders, the men and women with itching ears, never tired of new voices. They pilfer from their own churches the support of their presence and interest. When they summoned their pastor, they virtually pledged these as well as their money. It is genuine pilfering to withhold them.

But most of all does the gadder cheat himself. He loses the blessed home feeling, which makes one's own church a joyous foretaste of the Father's home awaiting us yonder. He loses the accumulating

Gadders

force of constantly recurring impressions. The varied preachers he hears may all be good, but they are good in different ways which neutralize each other, the sprightliness of one annulling the spirituality of another, the emotion of one driving out of mind the other's solid arguments. He cheats himself of strong church friendships. He steals away his repute among steady and sensible people. He classes himself with the human butterflies, none the less truly in flitting from church to church than if he flitted aimlessly from land to land.

"Gad, a troop shall overcome him," said the dying Jacob of one of his sons; and verily these gadders are overcome by a troop of follies, petulant criticisms, unsatisfied and half-recognized longings, the weariness of a search that ends ever with itself.

"But he shall overcome at the last," Jacob went on to say. May that prove true prophecy of every gadder!

An Insurance Against Shame

"My people shall never be ashamed."—*Joel* ii. 27.

TIMOROUS got great comfort from this verse when ague-smitten over a speech he had to make. "I belong to God's people," he argued. "I am working for God's glory. He will not let me be ashamed." Sure enough; the hands of his hearers clapped as vigorously as poor Timorous's knees had shaken together.

God's people will be ashamed to be ashamed. You see, they are not doing shameful things. And you see, their King never fails. Though His people sometimes seem to fail, it is all a part of His success. When the tide falls back, it is part of the same conquering ocean that will soon swing it forward again.

A man that has done his best, from

An Insurance Against Shame

right motives, has no right to be ashamed. For an honest Christian to fear that he will be ashamed is treason to Christ. The omnipotent hands to which you have confided yourself,—dare you think they will let you fall? The omniscient wisdom to which you have yielded your life-plans,— dare you think it will conduct them to failure?

(Ah, but if you have *not* confided, if you have *not* yielded!)

Get "holy boldness." *Un*holy boldness is about the most unholy thing on earth, but *holy* boldness is possible only by alliance with God in heaven. Take from "shame" its hissing sound, and "aim" is left. Aim at the right, make yourself one of God's people and seek solely His glory, and all hissing and fear of hissing will disappear from your life.

Out of Plumb

" Trust in the Lord with all thine heart: and lean not upon thine own understanding."—*Prov.* iii. 5 (Revised Version).

A BUILDING that is beginning to fall is not worth much, although it may be held up by a golden prop. A man that must lean is the less a man for that, although he lean on a jewel-headed cane. The Leaning Tower of Pisa holds up its head only because it is light in the upper story. No, after all has been said, every mason knows that safety lies in the plumb line, and not outside it.

Your intelligence is a fine thing, but if you lean on it, you and your fine thing will go down to the pit together. That is why you are so bowed down with worldly cares and frets and worries, brother; it is because you are leaning on your own understanding, and it is all bent, and crooked, and weak.

Out of Plumb

"But what is my understanding given me for?" I hear you ask. It is given you to straighten it up, to direct it toward heaven, to make it parallel with God's understanding; but not to lean upon. Isaiah heard God say, "I will make judgment the line, and righteousness the plummet" (xxviii. 17, Revised Version). Straighten up to *that*, and lean not upon your own understanding.

Ah, what a zest in living, when once you begin to let God manage your life! Head erect, now, for your leadership is on high. Feet buoyant, now, for the path is prepared before them. No more bending to a crutch, face reaching anxiously forward into the darkness. No more backache and narrow chest. You have joined the army of the Lord of hosts. His banner is waving over you. The music of His trumpets rings in your soul. Upright, downright, forthright, *forward march* for His victories!

A Genuine Klondike

" And the gold of that land is good."—*Gen.* ii. 12.

THE Bible has so much to say against the gold that is a root of all kinds of evil, that we are astonished to learn that the gold of *any* land is good.   Is there such a land now, in these days of trusts and monopolies and embezzlements and briberies and greed and pride?

Yes, there is.   The name of that land is Charis, which is Greek for Love, for Charity.   That is the only place where gold is good.

It isn't easy to stake out a claim there, or work a mine.   The country is all a lofty plateau, the table-land of High Thinking. It is hemmed in by steep and difficult mountains; the range is called Self-denial. You enter by Humility Pass, and it's a severe experience.   There is only one in-

A Genuine Klondike

habited spot in the entire region, namely, Service City. And the country is so lofty that all the rivers rush impetuously from it, so that floating in is quite out of the question.

But ah! how rich is the earth in Charis! Nuggets as big as a bushel basket are everyday affairs. Veins of the precious metal are as common as the veins in your body. And as for working the ore, the inhabitants simply "cast it upon the waters," and it is whirled off down the hills to the outer world. To come back again? Yes, after many days.

But the people that live in Charis are not worrying about their gold. The air is so clear and pure, and they are so strong and happy, that they dance singing to their mines, and the subterranean shafts and galleries echo all day to heavenly music. It is in that Land of Love, and there alone, that gold is good.

The Meaning of the Manger

"Ye shall find the babe lying in a manger."—
Luke ii. 12.

WHAT does the Christmas manger mean? That all of God's infinity can make a home for itself in my commonplaceness. That out of the dry straw of humdrum duties the Lord of the universe can build a throne. That since He was content with a manger, it is sin for me to fret in a mansion.

And now that God has appeared even there, shall I be surprised to find Him anywhere? If He would take up His abode with the beasts, may I not find some glimmer of Him among beastlike men? Dare I say of any life, however hard and forbidding, "There is no Christ there"? or of any task, however distasteful and unpromising, "I cannot find Christ in it"?

The Meaning of the Manger

Blessed Saviour, Thou of Bethlehem, Thou of Calvary, help me to make this a manger year. I will not seek Thee elsewhere, but just where I am. I will not defer Thee to some glorious day ahead, but I will have Thee to-day, and make that glorious. I will invite Thee into my stable, and ask Thee to help me sweep the floors and curry the horses and cut up the food for them, and I will draw Thee in among my rough stable companions. And at the end of the year, before the sun of next Christmas morning, my stable will have been transformed to a palace of the King, and the rough stablemen, and I among them, will have become King's sons. For that is Thy manger way.

Unseen Doorkeepers

" When they were past the first and the second ward, they came unto the iron gate that leadeth unto the city; which opened to them of his own accord."—*Acts* xii. 10.

OMETIMES we see the angel who opens to us the door of opportunity, but more often we do not see him, just as Peter did not see him. Sometimes God makes very plain to us the leading of His providence, but far more often things simply seem to happen " of their own accord."

Yet nothing happens of its own accord. No gate opens without the gate-opener. If any blessing has come into your life, you may be sure that *some one* put it there. If you hear any call, there is a mouth behind the voice. Not at haphazard has any opening of your life come to you;

Unseen Doorkeepers

some hand has taken down the bars, *some* arm has pushed back the doors.

The cloud of witnesses are more than witnesses : they are preparers; they are assistants. Your dead father is still helping you, if you will let him; your dead mother is still lifting your burdens. The angels are God's ministers sent on His errands, and what errand more pressing than to aid God's children?

When next you approach some closed door, whether it be closed by sickness or poverty or former failure or what not, do not see the door, do not think of it, but think only of the unseen angel waiting beside it. And remember : it is only by following the angels you see that you can obtain the good offices of the angels you do not see.

On Eagles' Wings

"Ye have seen what I did to the Egyptians, and how I bare you on eagles' wings, and brought you unto Myself."—*Ex.* xix. 4.

MAN is not much of a Christian until he is light-hearted. His happiness must not be studied, for some are actually happy—or think they are—from a sense of duty; but he will be happy because he cannot help it. His joy will leap and sing like a bird, exultant, spontaneous. It will need no forcing; it will force him into its sunny ways.

You cannot carry yourself into this overflowing happiness, any more than you can lift yourself by your boot-straps up to the skies. You must get God's wings under you. You must rest upon them. Not upon philosophy, not upon your own skill, not upon other men, not upon hu-

On Eagles' Wings

man institutions or contrivances, societies, books, schools, friends; not upon any earthly thing, but upon the eagles' wings.

And you must not expect them to bear you up to happiness, nor must it be with that desire that you summon them to you, but because you know God and want to know Him better; because you love God and want to love Him more. The wings are to bear you to Himself.

To be sure, you will find all joy there. To be sure, the wings will lift you into all clear vision. To be sure, the wings will bear you away from all the sorrows and pains of the world. But they will bear you to God! They will bear you to God!

God's Voice

"The glory of God came from the way of the east, and His voice was like a noise of many waters."—*Ezek.* xliii. 2.

I HAVE heard the masterful voice of the cataract, a voice that draws its majesty from a hundred hills; but I have heard in God's voice a tone more royal and commanding. The bursting of the tempest has gathered the elements into the fierceness of its down-pour, until its impetuous cry seemed to me like the wrath of the universe; but I have heard God's voice when it was more terrible than that. The soothing sound of the summer rain upon the dry roof and the leaves has often put me to sleep, as if it were a mother's lullaby; but the tender music of God's voice has brought me a rest still sweeter. The long anthem of the shore, with its chorus of dancing waves,

God's Voice

and its refrain always ending and always beginning, has allured my spirit out into the breadth of ocean,—its infinite variety, its boundless resources ; but when I stand by the ocean of God's love, and hear the anthem of His voice, it is like the song of all good men and angels, of all time and all eternity, of all wisdom and might and beneficence, yea, all sounds of power and holy meaning, of lovers and wives and mothers and little children, of statesmen and heroes, of saints and martyrs, of the Christ Himself,—all are in that single voice.

It is not one alone of these voices that has captured me in this noise of many waters,—not the sparkle of the brook, or the sweep of the river, or the thunder of the cataract, or the peaceful shower, or the many-minded ocean ; but it is all of them together, and many voices beside, for who that has really heard the voice of God can ever cease to hear it ?

God's Hilltops

" The Lord will make me to walk upon my high places."—*Hab.* iii. 19.

THE joy of the hills! To rise slowly, musingly, over the upland meadows into the still air; to get up on a level with the tree-tops and begin to see their green billows; to press on through hushed woods, up over the mossy ledges; to come out upon the clear summit, draw a long breath, and salute the world at your feet! Has nature a purer, more invigorating joy than this?

No, but God has; God, who is over nature. It is only on rare gala days that the hills are yours; rarer still, the mountains. Your life lies down among the bricks, and stretches along the pavements. Instead of the hillside hush and the hill-

God's Hilltops

top ecstasy, you have the rattle of carts and the confusion of many cares.

But at any time, even from the midst of these, God can make you to walk upon your high places. Up, up, up, He can lead you, out of the clash and the heat and the fretfulness, out of the poverty and the failure and the grief, up, up, up, to a place above all distraction, hushed with the peace of God ; above all seething annoyances, cool with the comfort of God ; above dark failure and grief, sunny with God's confidence and God's promises. From any valley, however low, even from the valley of the shadow of death, God can uplift His high places, and invite you to the summit.

I will not tell you what God's high places are, for you know already. Nor will I tell you how to find them, for you have been there ; but alas, how seldom !

Burdens and no Burdens

"My burden is light."—*Matt.* xi. 30.

AS Christ's burden light? "Now is My soul troubled." "Father, save Me from this hour." "Remove this cup from Me." "Why hast Thou forsaken Me?" No, it was not light. All the burdens that men's backs and men's hearts have groaned under since the world was, would make no such burden as our Lord's.

And the disciple is not above his Master. Christ's vast burden is not laid upon us; but we are not as strong as He. Yet what right have we to expect burdens that, *for us*, will be lighter than His were for Him?

Ah, His *were* light for Him, after all; and because His were light for Him, ours may be light for us. Probably I have

Burdens and no Burdens

quoted all that Christ said about His burden in all the Gospels. He did not call Himself the Burden-Bearer, but the Shepherd, the Physician, the Vine, the Way. He was supremely happy. He had no higher wish than that His joy might be in us.

That was because He and His burden were alike buoyed up by the Father's will. The earth would be a heavy thing to carry; but commit it to God's ether and His gravitation, and it carries itself and us. The earth's sin and woe make a weary weight; even Christ, the true Atlas, staggered under it,—staggered for an instant now and then till He felt Himself in the current of God's will, swept triumphantly around the Sun of Righteousness.

Thus, O Christ, Thou great Burden-Bearer who didst bear no burdens, teach me likewise so to dispose the weight Thou dost lay upon me that it may become firmament beneath my feet.

The Only Thing that Counts

"Amaziah did that which was right in the sight of the Lord, but not with a perfect heart." —2 *Chron.* xxv. 2.

"The high places were not taken away out of Israel: nevertheless the heart of Asa was perfect all his days."—2 *Chron.* xv. 17.

IT is not a matter of indifference with God what men accomplish, provided their hearts are right. The artist cares which way the tool runs, and not merely that it be obedient to his hand. The general cares about the result of the battle, and not merely that his soldiers carry out his orders. There is an outward, practical, tangible kingdom of God, as well as the kingdom of God which is within us. God rejoiced over Amaziah's right deeds, and mourned over Asa's failures.

But over *Amaziah* He mourned, and over *Asa* He rejoiced.

The Only Thing that Counts

I was teaching my child to print letters. It would have been a delight to me if her A had had less resemblance to a shoestring and her E to a ramroad; but the dear little hands were doing their best, and though I was not satisfied with her alphabet, I was satisfied with *her*.

And so let me learn to look upon the things I do or fail to do quite impersonally, as the Father looks at them. They count, but they do not count for me or against me. They please God or displease Him, but they have nothing to do with *my* pleasing God or displeasing Him. If my heart is right with God, I am right with God. All of me. Right altogether. Right, perfect, with no subtraction whatever on account of my blundering, thwarted deeds. Thy kingdom come within me; Thy will be done within me; make my heart perfect toward Thee, O God, that Thou mayst keep me in perfect peace.

Exaltation

"And I, if I be lifted up from the earth, will draw all men unto Me."—*John* xii. 32.

"IF I be executed, I will draw all men to My scaffold!" That, in modern equivalent, is what Christ said of His crucifixion. Probably a more startling statement was never made in this world; and the most startling point about it has been its literal and growing fulfillment.

Christ never spoke of His humiliation as a humiliation, but as an exaltation: "If I be *lifted up.*" He was not going down into the valley of the shadow, but up on the lordly mountain,—Mount Calvary. At the outset of His ministry the Adversary had taken Him to a very high mountain, whence He saw all the kingdoms of the world. Now at the close of His ministry He was lifted up to a height

Exaltation

whence He saw, with Pisgah vision, that the kingdoms would all be His. And that summit of glory was the climax of grief.

Influence comes only through suffering. " Drawing power " is only toward crosses. The true leaders of men count no sorrow an evil, if it brings them into a wider sympathy; no persecution a misfortune, if it raises them nearer God. Are you ambitious? Do you long—and rightfully —for power with men? Go, get yourself crucified with Christ, and you will have all the influence possible for men to exert.

Asking that Wins

"Ask, and it shall be given you."—*Matt.*
vii. 7.

THERE is a way of talking about
receiving Christ that leads only
to disappointment; a way that
makes it seem far too easy:
"You have only to ask, and Christ will
come into your lives for the asking."

It is true that Christ is far more eager
to enter our lives than we are to receive
Him; true that He awaits only the asking. *But what asking!*

The asking of the lips, which must not
only move in easy petition, but must con-
fess His name at all times before men, and
spread abroad His praises.

The asking of the hands, which must
not only be raised in supplication, but be
outstretched, palm downward, in generous
giving.

46

Asking that Wins

The asking of the feet, which must not only rise on the mount of vision, but descend into the valley of service; yea, go to the ends of the earth, at bidding of the Voice.

The asking of the mind, which must be at one with Christ's mind not only in this matter of His coming but in all other matters, proudly recognizing no wisdom except the Teacher's.

The asking of the will, which must not only be bent on drawing Christ to itself, but be passionately determined to throw itself utterly at the feet of Christ.

The asking of the heart, which not only must long for Christ, but must, in the comparison, long for nothing else,—not for gold, nor fame, nor ease, nor men's applause, nor worldly success, nor even human love.

Have you yet asked for Christ?

Abiding Success

UCCESS is getting the best thing possible. In the days of Joshua it was the Law, the Book. In our day, it is Him whom the Book discloses, it is Christ.

When a man fails, it is because he lacks Christ. If he would transmute his failure into success, there is only one way to do it : let him get Christ. To study successful lives will not do it, unless such study lead them to the Life. To cultivate determination will not do it, unless he wins Christ, who alone can control the will. Dogged toil will not do it, shining brilliancy will not do it ; nothing but Christ can make a man successful.

If you are a failure, in one point or in all points, look honestly, and you will see that it is for want of something Christ

Abiding Success

alone can supply. You need His firmness,
or His purity, or His clear insight into the
future, or His knowledge of real values, or
His obedience, or His courage, or His
sympathy and tact. Possibly you need
His acquiescence in apparent failure, if it
seems to be God's way, certain that along
His way alone comes the sure success.
Whatever you need, you need Christ.
And when once you have gained Christ,
you will know that your life is a success,
for time and for eternity.

Good Men to Avoid

"Meddle not with them that are given to change."—*Prov.* xxiv. 21.

MUCH of the stability of our lives depends upon our friends. The boulder on the shore is the sport of every wave; but fasten it with other rocks in a granite friendship, and base them all on the solid rock bottom, and you have a lighthouse which the waves cannot conquer. If your friends are the double-minded men, you will be driven by the wind and tossed with them. If your friends are unstable as water, you also will not prevail.

Friendship is spiritual dependence on a man. You may be surrounded by men, numberless as the waves of the sea, who are inconstant as these waves, and you will not be hurt by their inconstancy if

Good Men to Avoid

you are independent of them. They may be true to high ideals to-day and false to them to-morrow; but your loyalty will remain firm. They may be cheerful this minute and frowning or weeping the next; but your peace will flow as a river. You are anchored outside of their moods.

But if you have made them your friends! If every change of their barometer is reflected in your soul, and you are uplifted by their bliss only to fall with their gloom, and ennobled by their faithfulness only to be smirched by their sin; if such a man, such a woman, has been admitted within the charmed circle of your life influences, has perhaps even become your lover, or your wife, or your husband, alas for you, and alas for your life!

The only guard against inconstancy is aloofness from the inconstant. And that, also, is the only way to help them. You cannot stand on the water and lift another man.

A Mouth Enlarged

"My mouth is enlarged."—1 *Sam.* ii. 1.

CERTAINLY Hannah was a beautiful woman. Certainly we have a right to fancy her eyes of the brightest, her face of the fairest, her lips of the sweetest. And I am quite sure that although her mouth may have been the daintiest among Hebrew women, yet this phrase from her song of thanksgiving pictures for us the chief feature in her loveliness.

Ah, sister, you may have the most tender and loving of hearts, but no one will know it unless your mouth is enlarged to tender and loving words. Ah, brother, you may think you are the child of God, but others are not likely to think so, and I doubt whether God is likely to think so, unless your mouth is enlarged to praise God.

For it is true that usually noble feelings

A Mouth Enlarged

will compel noble words, and a large heart will enlarge the mouth in the same way Hannah's lovely mouth was enlarged. Silence is not golden, it is pewter, where speech has any righteous work to do. A little mouth goes with a little soul,—a mouth so little that great thoughts cannot get out of it, thoughts of generosity, thoughts of unselfishness, thoughts of sacrifice, thoughts of appreciation, of gratitude, of helpfulness, of worship, of soul-winning. O God, open Thou my lips, and my mouth shall show forth Thy praise!

Undying Ardor

"The fire shall ever be burning upon the altar."—*Lev*. vi. 13.

E are no longer called to maintain perpetual fire on a literal altar. God's altar, we say, is now the human heart. The sacrifice He desires is a ready will. The sacrificial tools are hands and feet, and all the instruments of living. The flame is the fire of Pentecost.

This is true; but let us take heed, or in spiritualizing the symbols we shall lose sight of the reality. To worship God in the spirit is always harder than to yield the service of the flesh. Easier is it to care for a thousand temples,—gatekeepers, doorkeepers, courses of priests, incense, basins, snuffers and tongs, purifications, anointings, ceremonies unending,—than to care for a single heart. To let the fire

54

upon the brazen altar go out, and say, " God dwelleth not in temples made with hands," is no release of burden ; it is the assumption of a vast responsibility, a glorious privilege. For we, not made with hands, become at once His only temple.

" Pray without ceasing, praise without ceasing ! "—ah, Lord, how have Thy modern altars grown cold ! How have Thy temple servants grown careless ! En-kindle the flames anew with fire from heaven ! Our desires shall feed them, our ambitions, our pleasures, our gains. When we wake in the night, we will heap the fluel higher. In the pauses of our tasks we will replenish it. We will hold it ready for any sacrifice ; yea, ready for the coming of the Temple-Lord Himself.

Why We Pray

"Because He hath inclined His ear unto me, therefore will I call upon Him as long as I live." —*Psa.* cxvi. 2.

THAT is strange reasoning. We might have expected it to read : "Because He hath inclined His ear unto me, therefore will I praise Him," or, "therefore will I serve Him in return ; " but the Psalmist better understood the true relation between God and man : "Because He hath answered many prayers, I will offer many more ; because He hath given me much, I will continue to ask great things of Him ; because He hath been kind, I will give Him an opportunity to be more gracious still."

And that is the way God likes to be treated,—not as a bargain-driver, so many blessings for so much service; not as a miser, niggardly of His gifts; but as the

Why We Pray

being He is, the most lavishly generous being in the universe, the Giver who makes no conditions : "Take all you will, freely, without money and without price ; have it for the asking,—your pockets full, your hands full, your arms full, and next time bring a bigger basket ! "

Never think that because God has granted you a blessing, you must wait awhile before you importune Him again. Never think that you must weigh your petitions, lest they seem exorbitant. Never think that you must accumulate a stock of good deeds, which you may take to barter at the heavenly storehouse.

You are a pauper, but as a newborn babe is a pauper. And the Father is never so happy as when He can supply the need of His child.

Other Folks' Buildings

" And Hiram sent to Solomon, saying, . . .
' I will do all thy desire, . . . and thou
shalt accomplish my desire.' "—1 *Kings* v. 8, 9.

IRAM seemed quite as much in-
terested in Solomon's temple as
if it were his own. Its lofty
walls did not depress him, or
cast a shadow over his spirit. Tyre was
none the poorer because Jerusalem was en-
riched. Hiram had learned how to annex
kingdoms by rejoicing in their prosperity.

And now let me consider carefully with
myself what are the life purposes of those
nearest me, and how I am aiding them, or
whether I am aiding them at all. How
easy it is for me to become absorbed in my
great intentions and forget that others have
any great intentions, or indeed that they
have anything at all to do in the world except to help me in my undertakings ! In-

Other Folks' Buildings

stead of widening my interests out into theirs, I would cram their lives into mine, which is already too much crowded. Instead of opening my windows to their sunshine, I bid them draw their curtains in sympathy with my gloom.

When I testily assume that my own life purpose is so immeasurably superior in worth and grandeur to those of all the people around me that their time and energies are freely to be given to aid me while no aid is given in return,— that is proof that my life purpose is not worthy, but ignoble. I will no longer defeat myself by selfishness. I will give up a part of my time, regularly and generously, to the work of others that is foreign to my own. I will rejoice in their success as in my own; nay, I will make it my own also. I will accomplish their desire, and they—though I shall take less heed—will accomplish mine.

A Possible Possession

" Let this mind be in you, which was also in Christ Jesus."—*Phil.* ii. 5.

IF you could know that a piece of wood lying before you was a portion of the very cross on which Christ suffered, with what reverence would you gaze upon it! If you could hold in your hands for a single minute an actual bit of carpenter work He had made, how impossible it would be henceforth for those hands to do anything mean or unkind or base! And if—the very thought is one hardly to be entertained—you could wear for a day that seamless robe, what royal adornment but would seem ignoble in comparison! If a nation owned any one of these things, no wealth in its treasury would be so valued, and no distinction would be so honorable as to be custodian of the precious relic.

A Possible Possession

But any one may gain for his very own a possession beside which the Holy Grail itself would be trivial and unmeaning—he may gain the mind of Christ.

Until this thought of Christ's mind has come to have for us a reality more solid and sensible than the cloth and wood and stone we handle, religion has little reality for us. Until the thought of getting Christ's mind has seized us with a practical vividness as actual to our conception as the gaining of dollars to a business man or the winning of a new empire to Napoleon, Christianity has slight hold upon us.

How blessed to have Christ living in my house! I can have Him living in my house. To have Him working in my office! He will be glad to work in my office. For the mind of Christ is Christ Himself, the most real of all realities; and no way I could ever express the reality of His possible presence can make it seem more real to me than it is.

Even so come, Lord Jesus!

Vipers and Tasks

"When Paul had gathered a bundle of sticks
. . . there came a viper."—*Acts* xxviii. 3.

IF the service of God were easy, it would not be worth rewarding. Hidden away in every task there is a viper. It may be a stinging worry or a weary ache, the mischievous hiss of some alluring pleasure, or the fang of some poisonous doubt. The viper will not hurt us, if we take hold of our task in the fear of God; it will drop harmless from our hand. But if we grasp our task impatiently, with arrogant assumption, with weak self-pity, in an instant the fangs strike and the poison enters.

There are some who will not gather sticks for fear of snakes, and so there is no fire in their lives, no brightness, no warmth, no energy. All forests are transparent to their keen eyes,—without leaves,

Vipers and Tasks

without flowers, without tree-boles, nothing but serpents. Mention an undertaking, and at once they spy the viper in it. "No one will thank you." "It will be an endless piece of work." "I doubt whether it can be done." "Is it worth doing, anyway?" And at a viper's hiss the man flees.

Be a manlier spirit mine, O Father, who workest hitherto and dost protect all workers! Let me not shrink from any log on which Thou dost lay my hand. Obedience is antidote for all venom. Each glittering serpent I meet in Thy way but adds a gleam to my crown. I shall fear no evil, when Thou art with me. Thy rod and Thy staff shall strike all vipers down.

Sycomore Trees

" Zaccheus . . . because he was little of stature . . . climbed up into a sycomore tree to see Him."—*Luke* xix. 2–4.

ITTLE men and women, all of us! mere pygmies beside the great things to see and learn and do! And the mistake made by many men is that they think they must reach everything from their own feet. Whatever their tiptoeing cannot attain unto, they think is not for them.

The wise man knows, on the contrary, that God has filled the world with trees, on purpose to help out the altitude of little men. If you are ignorant, get on top of some tree of knowledge. If you are weak and sinful, there is the tree of Calvary; draw yourself up to it. If you are sick, there is the tree that is for the healing of the nations.

Sycomore Trees

God has placed our felicity up among those branches, a golden fruit. Out of reach ? Yes, from the ground ; but there is the trunk and there are the branches. The sycomore will be a tree of life, but only to them that lay hold upon it.

You never had a task to which you were equal ; no man ever had. Though it be only to draw a pail of water, God must furnish nerve and muscle, bone-lever and brain-incentive, flowing elements and gravitative force. If you would draw a man to God, is God less likely to afford the means ?

It is no miracle that Deity should furnish trees by which we can climb over all obstacles ; the miracle is that we can climb. By the side of every difficulty He has set a tree of power,—not my power, but His ; and all I have to do is to ascend into it. And shall I be content to remain a groundling ?

The Wonderful

"For unto us a child is born . . . and His name shall be called Wonderful."—*Isa*. ix. 6.

DO you know the list of the seven wonders of the world? One was a lighthouse, but Christ is the Light of the world. One was the pyramids, but Christ is the Apex of all glorious summits. One was a statue, but Christ is the express Image of God's person. One was a Colossus, but Christ overtops all giants. One was a hanging garden, but Christ is the true Vine. One was a temple, but Christ is mightier than all temples,—could destroy them and rebuild them in three days or three minutes. One was a mausoleum, but Christ is the Life.

It is easy, in the admirable maze of created things, to let our admiration wander without reaching the Creator. It is easy

The Wonderful

to be so in love with our work as to disregard the Infinite Lover, who has given us the petty tasks that we call great, and designs through them only to draw us nearer Himself. It is easy to be so engrossed with the work of other men, so tangled in their toil, as to forget the Redeemer of mankind.

I will make that mistake no longer. For even when my life was busiest, that error has stripped it of interest, torn it from romance and beauty, and dragged it down into the whirling dust. I will rise to be with Thee, O Thou Wonderful! All the marvels of grass and tree and cloud and sun shall be only a ladder up to Thee. Whatever the times may crowd upon me, I shall take time for Thee, O Thou that inhabitest eternity!

Tributaries

"Woe unto you, when all men shall speak well of you!"—*Luke* vi. 26.

THERE was once a river, fed by beautiful mountain streams. Its waters were clear as crystal, and artists came to paint it, and poets sung its praises. But the river was fond of receiving tribute as it went on its way through the world. A great muddy pond offered it a gift, and it took the gift, —a mass of dirty water that destroyed all the transparency of the lovely stream. Farther on, a filthy town along its banks made proffer of a present, and the foolish river was flattered into acceptance. It received to itself, therefore, a burden of impurities that made its waters bad-smelling and unhealthy. So it went on, until the river became a by-word for foulness and ugliness. "Alas!" it cried, as it

68

strove to wash its slimy current in the great, clean ocean, "how silly I was to accept tribute from everybody!"

For the acceptance of praise means more than the acknowledgment of blame. Blame is a physician, who departs with the disease; but praise is a friend who abides. If you shake hands with every man, before long your hands will be soiled, and sooner or later you will have the smallpox. More poisons enter lives through flattery than through calumny.

Yet how we shrink from blame, scrutinize it with hate, fight against it in terror! And how greedily we welcome praise,— praise from any source, so it be approval! Let me transfer that welcome to blame, for it may be medicinal; and that scrutiny to praise. Let me suspect men's applause, and entertain it coldly in my heart. Let me assure myself that no praise is safe for me but God's "Well done!" and even that is not deserved.

Wayside Witnessing

"In all thy ways acknowledge Him, and He shall direct thy paths."—*Prov.* iii. 6.

YOU may only be going to the grocery to get a pound of butter. Never mind. Along that way, if you look sharply, there will surely be some opportunity to acknowledge God. Bowing on the street to that poor woman may be made as much an acknowledgment of God as bowing in prayer at church. You cannot go down stairs without having a chance to acknowledge Him. It may be by a snatch of cheery song. It may be by a merry hail or thoughtful inquiry, a word of sympathy or of praise. Keep your eyes open, Christian, as you walk along these ways of earth, and you will see chances of acknowledging God more numerous than the telephone poles, or the hitching-posts, or the signs above the shop-doors.

A reaping machine proudly bears its maker's name, and so it acknowledges him not only on the harvest field, but on the way thither; yes, and when laid up for the winter. Whoever looks upon it, whether it is in rest or motion, and whether wheat is near it or not, knows the name of the maker that was its owner's choice.

And so whoever wears, definitely and frankly, the name of Christ, preaches a sermon as long as his daily walk, and sings through every conversation an anthem of praise. He cannot pray, even, but it will be to the glory of God.

And of course, if thus we walk with God, we cannot go astray, for God is not going astray. He directs our paths by directing His own.

www.ingramcontent.com/pod-product-compliance
Lightning Source LLC
Chambersburg PA
CBHW020250090426
42735CB00010B/1868